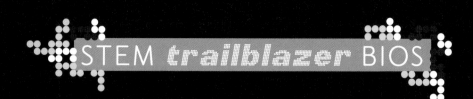

STEM *trailblazer* BIOS

CODE-BREAKER AND MATHEMATICIAN

ALAN TURING

BY HEATHER E. SCHWARTZ

Lerner Publications ◆ Minneapolis

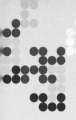

Lerner Publications Company
A division of Lerner Publishing Group, Inc.
241 First Avenue North
Minneapolis, MN 55401 USA

For reading levels and more information, look up this title at www.lernerbooks.com.

Content consultant: John Dooley, professor of computer science, Knox College

Library of Congress Cataloging-in-Publication Data

Names: Schwartz, Heather E., author.
Title: Code-breaker and mathematician Alan Turing / by Heather E. Schwartz.
Description: Minneapolis : Lerner Publications, [2017] | Series: STEM trailblazer bios | Audience:
    Ages 7–11. | Audience: Grade 4 to 6.
Identifiers: LCCN 2017010166 (print) | LCCN 2017024181 (ebook) | ISBN 9781512499834 (eb pdf) |
    ISBN 9781512499803 (lb : alk. paper)
Subjects: LCSH: Turing, Alan Mathison, 1912-1954—Juvenile literature. | Mathematicians—
    Great Britain—Biography—Juvenile literature. | Gay men—Great Britain—Biography—Juvenile
    literature. | Enigma cipher system—Juvenile literature.
Classification: LCC QA29.T8 (ebook) | LCC QA29.T8 S39 2017 (print) | DDC 510.92 [B] —dc23
LC record available at https://lccn.loc.gov/2017010166

Manufactured in the United States of America
1-43616-33367-6/7/2017

The images in this book are used with the permission of: © REX/Shutterstock, p. 4; © London Metropolitan Archives, City of London/Bridgeman Images, p. 5; © The Turing Digital Archive/King's College London, p. 6; Courtesy of the Sherborne School, pp. 7, 8; © National Physical Laboratory/Crown Copyright/Science Source, p. 10; © Private Collection/Prismatic Pictures/Bridgeman Images, p. 11; Library of Congress (HABS NJ,11-PRINT,4B--1), p. 13; Sueddeutsche Zeitung Photo/Alamy Stock Photo, p. 14; National Archives (200-SFF-52), p. 16; Chronicle/Alamy Stock Photo, p. 17; © Christian Lendl/flickr.com (CC BY 2.0), p. 18; Photo courtesy Dr. David Hamer/National Museum of the US Air Force, p. 19; Les Wilson/SOLO Syndication/Newscom, p. 21; World History Archive/Alamy Stock Photo, p. 22; © Science & Society Picture Library/Getty Images, pp. 23, 25; Mike Robinson/Alamy Stock Photo, p. 27; © National Portrait Gallery, London, UK/Prismatic Pictures/Bridgeman Images, p. 28.

Front cover: © Private Collection/Prismatic Pictures/Bridgeman Images.

Main body text set in Adrianna Regular 13/22. Typeface provided by Chank.

CONTENTS

Chapter 1

Alan Turing poses with friends in 1939.

BUDDING
BRILLIANCE

Mathematician Alan Turing showed that ideas could be as powerful as weapons. Combining his math and science talents with a passion to help his country, he found a way to help Britain and its allies win World War II (1939–1945).

Alan was born in London, England, on June 23, 1912. Alan's parents soon went back to India, where Alan's father worked for the government. Alan and his brother did not live with their parents. The boys lived with family friends and grew up in England.

London, England, in 1912

Alan began attending Hazelhurst, a boarding school in Sussex, when he was nine years old. He lived and studied there. Alan loved math and science, and he spent most of his free time thinking about the subjects. He even did his own chemistry experiments. But his abilities were often unrecognized by his teachers and classmates.

Alan's brother, John, also went to school at Hazelhurst.

Hockey
or
Watching the Daisies
Grow

Alan's mother sketched this picture of Alan (*left*) examining daisies while his classmates played a field hockey game. Young Alan was always more interested in plants than in sports.

Alan was especially fascinated with plants. Alan's mother sketched a picture of him gazing at daisies while he was supposed to be playing field hockey with Hazelhurst classmates. Alan also enjoyed reading a book called *Natural Wonders Every Child Should Know* by Edwin Tenney Brewster. It was a well-known science book that covered the similarities and differences between living things.

Alan's mother was not pleased that her son enjoyed science so much. Science was not considered a proper course of study for young British gentlemen. Schools at the time valued subjects such as Latin and English literature. She worried he would not be accepted into a good school after leaving Hazelhurst.

DIFFICULT STUDENT

His mother had no reason to worry. At thirteen, Alan was accepted to the Sherborne School, a well-regarded British institution. There, he kept digging into his interest in science on his own. He read Albert Einstein's general theory of relativity. The theory was Einstein's idea of

This photo was taken when Alan was a student at Sherborne School. The school is in southwestern England.

how gravity works. He said that objects bend, or curve, time and space depending on how much mass they have. Gravity is the result of these curves. Despite the complex nature of the theory, Alan's notes on the subject proved that he understood it.

Alan was clearly intelligent. But his teachers didn't see it. They called his schoolwork careless and sloppy, and he was so far behind in some subjects that he almost wasn't allowed to take his final exams.

PROVING HIMSELF

But Alan took his exams. He passed and graduated from Sherborne School. Then he went to King's College in Cambridge. His teachers there were more accepting of his interest in math and science. He began to think about more complex mathematical ideas, such as **statistics**. Turing rowed, sailed, and ran to clear his mind when he wasn't studying.

After graduating in 1934, Turing stayed at the college as a **fellow**—a scholar who works at a college. He studied **probability** theory. This branch of mathematics has to do with how likely it is that random events will occur. In 1936, Turing won a Smith's Prize from the University of Cambridge for his work in probability theory.

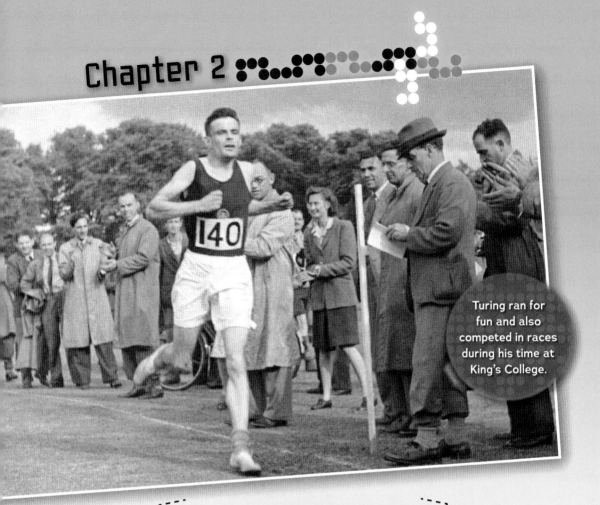

Chapter 2

Turing ran for fun and also competed in races during his time at King's College.

CODE-BREAKING

Turing was out running one day when he got an idea he just had to write down. He thought it might be possible to build a computing machine that could solve math problems by itself.

Turing imagined his machine reading a set of instructions for solving math problems. The instructions would be on a length of tape. The tape would have squares on it. Some squares would be blank. Others would be marked with characters such as 1 or 0. The machine would read the numbers on the tape and be able to calculate answers to difficult problems.

Turing was one of the world's first computer scientists.

The machine Turing had in mind was a thought experiment. He didn't think it could really be built. He worked alone and didn't realize other mathematicians were working on similar ideas.

In 1936, Turing published a paper about a math problem. To solve the problem, he wrote about a computing machine. The paper was the first explanation of how such a machine could be programmed. He didn't know it then, but the paper would be groundbreaking in the world of mathematics.

PREPARING FOR WAR

The same year he published his paper, Turing began

COMPUTER PIONEER

Turing's idea for instructions for a computing machine is the basis for modern computer languages. Most computer languages are translated by the machine into a series of 1s and Os called a binary code. By reading the order of the binary code, the computer can follow complex instructions.

attending Princeton University in New Jersey. He studied mathematics and, later, **cryptography**. His interest in cryptography grew from frightening current events during the 1930s.

Princeton University is one of the oldest colleges in the United States. It began accepting students in 1746.

Adolf Hitler (*right*) became the leader of Germany in 1933.

While Turing was studying at King's College and Princeton, Adolf Hitler rose to power to become the dictator of Germany. Hitler and the Nazi Party had plans to expand into other countries through military force. Britain was likely to go to war against Germany. Like many others throughout Europe and the world, Turing was scared. But he knew that knowledge of cryptography could be useful in a war.

In 1938, Turing graduated from Princeton. He was offered a position at the university and could have stayed in the United States. Instead, he returned to Cambridge and then began work at the Government Code and Cypher School. It wasn't really a school but rather a secret code-breaking organization started during World War I (1914–1918). It gathered intelligence about the enemy to keep Britain safe.

The Germans **enciphered** their military messages. That prevented their enemies from reading them and learning their plans. In 1938, a team of mathematicians in Poland designed a machine called Bomba. It **deciphered** codes and allowed the mathematicians to unlock and read entire coded messages written by the German military. It worked as long as the Germans followed a certain pattern when creating their messages each day.

Soon enough, the Germans changed their method of creating codes so Bomba could not crack them. Bomba would still prove to be useful, however. It would become an important part of Turing's code-breaking work during World War II.

TECH TALK

"[Turing] invented the idea of software, essentially. It's software that's really the important invention."

—*Freeman Dyson, physicist*

Chapter 3

Germany invaded Poland using a tactic called blitzkrieg, or lightning war.

BUILDING
THE BOMBE

On September 1, 1939, Germany invaded Poland. Two days later, France and Britain declared war on Germany. World War II had begun. Turing's work in math and cryptography suddenly became urgent and an important part of the war effort.

Britain and its allies, including the United States, wanted to decode Germany's messages to prevent surprise attacks. But the Germans had a secret weapon on their side: the Enigma machine. Invented by a German engineer, the Enigma machine could encipher code that was impossible for human code-breakers to crack.

German soldiers encipher messages on an Enigma machine during World War II.

The Enigma machine looked similar to a typewriter—machines with keyboards that people used to write on before computers were developed. It had a keyboard and several rotating wheels. When messages were typed on the keyboard, the wheels turned and changed letters to scramble messages. The machine was able to scramble letters in so many different ways that code-breakers could not possibly try them all. And the settings were changed each day to create an entirely new code.

GUESSING GAME

Turing had some clues about how to crack the Enigma code.

Messages scrambled by an Enigma machine could be easily unscrambled only by another Enigma machine.

He knew that certain words and phrases were common in messages the Germans sent. For example, many messages were about the weather. Commonly used words such as *wettervorhersage*, or weather forecast, could be deciphered. These were called cribs. A crib can help unlock the rest of the text in a message.

By studying captured German intelligence, Turing also learned that the Enigma machine would never encipher a letter as itself. It would always be a different letter in a scrambled message. The Germans made their machine work this way on purpose, thinking it would make the messages harder to unscramble. But knowing a letter would never be coded as itself was a clue that Turing used to create cribs.

```
1827  3225XM  C1626  W987
SEXTO




H6R  5RH DE C  1346 = 3TLE  = 2TL  224 = HUW XNG  =
DKRKI   CUZAF   MNSDC   AWXVJ   DVZNH   DMOZN   NWRJC   KKJQO
ELWIK   XDUUF   ECEGN   OUNNQ   CIIZX   FUTXF   BTNWI   GOECK
CMYUC   KTTYB   ZMDTU   WCNWH   OXOFX   ERVQW   JUCVY   PQACQ
EBMXE   NOQKF   LWRWR   LGKXZ   BPYWR   GQVYG   WJDGA   QXKVC
MQQJJ   PVSLG   WFZJZ   HHWQG   YFCQQ   RMVRR   QQIDQ   QVVIW
LJLBH   LHHDI   OFWUY   JJQGX   BWPZ
CCT  2/3  RCXGN
1852 FLC
```

Scrambled German messages such as this one were commonly intercepted by British agents.

These clues helped Turing make educated guesses about how the Enigma code could be cracked. They were bits of information that helped form a mathematical solution in his mind. But they were not enough to break the code.

CRACKING THE CODE

The main obstacle to cracking the Enigma code was the number of possibilities that existed. There were too many for a code-breaker to test. But Turing believed a machine could do what humans could not.

He built a machine called the Bombe based on the Polish Bomba. The Bombe was made of rotors and switches that acted like thirty-six Enigma machines. The parts moved quickly to test thousands of different letter combinations.

THE BOMBE

The Bombe was an enormous machine. It was about 7 feet (2.1 m) wide, 6.5 feet (2 m) tall, and weighed 1 ton (0.9 t). It used 12 miles (19 km) of wiring and contained ninety-seven thousand parts.

To ensure that British agents would be able to decipher all the German messages they intercepted, more than two hundred Bombes were built during the war.

With the help of a crib, the Bombe worked on German messages that the British intercepted. It found a small number of likely solutions to each enciphered message for code-breakers to check. From there, they could easily decipher the code and read the messages.

Chapter 4

People in London celebrate V-E day, or Victory in Europe Day, on May 8, 1945.

AFTER THE WAR

World War II ended with Germany's defeat in 1945. The Bombe played a major role in the outcome. Messages deciphered by the Bombe told about the enemy's movements and plans. Some experts believe the fighting would have continued for two more years without Turing's Bombe. They estimate two million more people would have died in the war.

Britain recognized Turing's efforts. He was honored as an Officer of the Most Excellent Order of the British Empire. After the war, he continued working in his field. At the National Physical Laboratory in London, Turing designed the Automatic Computing Engine. It was the first computer design that could store digital programs.

Turing's Automatic Computing Engine was first put to use in 1950.

THE TURING TEST

In 1948, Turing became deputy director of the Computing Machine Laboratory at the University of Manchester. There, he developed ideas for computer software and artificial intelligence. He created the Turing test to study artificial intelligence.

The Turing test was an experiment to see if a computer's artificial intelligence could really think for itself. A person acting as a judge received messages on a computer screen. Some messages came from another person. Others were from the computer. If the judge mistakenly believed the computer-generated messages came from a human at least half the time, it could be assumed that the computer was intelligent. Forms of the Turing test are still used to judge a computer's thinking ability.

TECH TALK

"A computer would deserve to be called intelligent if it could deceive a human into believing that it was human."

—Alan Turing

Turing (*right*) works with fellow computer scientists in 1951. He was also interested in biology, chemistry, and other sciences.

FINAL CONTRIBUTIONS

In 1952, Turing turned his attention to biology and how things grow. His interest in the subject went back to his childhood, when he'd been fascinated with plants. As an adult, he had new ideas that explained how patterns in living things develop mathematically. He published a paper on his ideas, focusing on daisies.

Around this time, Turing's work was interrupted. In England in the 1950s, it was against the law to be homosexual. Turing was homosexual. In 1952, he was convicted of the crime of being homosexual. He lost his security clearance. He could no longer work in cryptography for the government.

DEATH AND HONOR

Turing died of cyanide poisoning in June 1954. Many people believe he committed suicide. But his death may have been accidental. Turing often used cyanide in experiments at home. He may have swallowed the poison or inhaled its vapors by mistake.

After his death, the British government recognized that Turing had been mistreated when he had been convicted of a crime.

TECH TALK

"I believe that at the end of the [twentieth] century the use of words and general educated opinion will have altered so much that one will be able to speak of machines thinking without expecting to be contradicted."

—*Alan Turing*

People may visit the Alan Turing Memorial in Manchester, England. It was unveiled in 2001.

In 2009, British prime minister Gordon Brown offered an official apology to Turing on behalf of the government. In 2013, Queen Elizabeth II formally pardoned him for his criminal conviction.

Turing continues to be honored and respected for his work. He helped save the world from Nazi aggression, and he sparked new ideas about math, science, and technology.

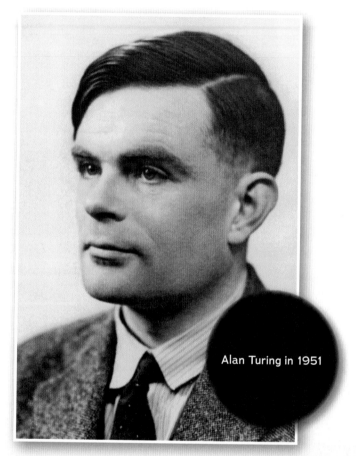

Alan Turing in 1951

TIMELINE

1912
Alan Turing is born.

1934
Turing graduates from King's College.

1938
Turing graduates from Princeton University.

1939
World War II begins.

1945
World War II ends.

1950
Turing develops the Turing test.

1952
Turing loses his security clearance after being convicted of a crime for being homosexual.

1954
Turing dies.

2009
Britain's prime minister officially apologizes to Turing.

2013
Queen Elizabeth II formally pardons Turing.

SOURCE NOTES

15 Joel Achenbach, "What 'The Imitation Game' Didn't Tell You about Turing's Greatest Triumph," *Washington Post*, February 20, 2015, http://www .washingtonpost.com/national/health-science/what-imitation-game-didnt-tell -you-about-alan-turings-greatest-triumph/2015/02/20/ffd210b6-b606-11e4 -9423-f3d0a1ec335c_story.html?utm_term=.bfb1ad33b44c.

24 S. Barry Cooper, "Alan Turing: 'I Am Building a Brain.' Half a Century Later, Its Successor Beat Kasparov," *Guardian* (US ed.), May 14, 2012, https://www .theguardian.com/uk/the-northerner/2012/may/14/alan-turing-gary-kasparov -computer.

26 "Quora Question: Can Intelligent Machines Mimic Sentience?," *Newsweek*, December 25, 2016, http://www.newsweek.com/quora-question-can -machines-become-sentient-535030?amp=1.

GLOSSARY

cryptography
the science of encoding or decoding information

deciphered
turned code into normal text

enciphered
turned normal text into code

fellow
a scholar who works at a college

probability
how likely something is to happen

statistics
the scientific study of large amounts of numerical data

FURTHER INFORMATION

BOOKS

Burrows, Terry. *Codes, Ciphers, and Cartography: Math Goes to War.* Minneapolis: Lerner Publications, 2018. Explore how math is used on the battlefield.

Kallen, Stuart A. *World War II Spies and Secret Agents.* Minneapolis: Lerner Publications, 2018. Read more about codes and secrets during World War II.

Nagelhout, Ryan. *Alan Turing: Master of Cracking Codes.* New York: PowerKids, 2016. Learn more about Turing's work in World War II and on computer development.

WEBSITES

Alan Turing Facts and Biography
http://www.facts-about.org.uk/famous-people-facts-starting -with-a/alan-turing.htm
Learn more about the life of Alan Turing.

Get the Math
http://www.thirteen.org/get-the-math
Visit this site to learn more about math and its practical uses.

National Security Agency—Cryptologic Machines Image Gallery
https://www.nsa.gov/resources/everyone/digital-media-center /image-galleries/cryptologic-museum/machines
Take a look at images of the Bombe and other coding machines.

LERNER

SOURCE

Expand learning beyond the printed book. Download free, complementary educational resources for this book from our website, www.lerneresource.com.

INDEX

ABOUT THE AUTHOR

Heather E. Schwartz has written more than sixty nonfiction books for kids. She always enjoys researching and learning about people with a passion for what they do, like Alan Turing.